Manta Rays

Tori Miller

PowerKiDS press.

New York

To Ryan, who loves fish

Published in 2009 by The Rosen Publishing Group, Inc.
29 East 21st Street, New York, NY 10010

First Edition

Editor: Joanne Randolph
Book Design: Greg Tucker
Photo Researcher: Jessica Gerweck

Photo Credits: Cover © Georgie Holland/age fotostock; p. 5 © Brian J. Skerry/Getty Images; pp. 7, 12–13 Shutterstock.com; p. 9 © Tim Laman/Getty Images; p. 11 © Peter Pinnock/Getty Images; p. 15 © Biosphoto/Kobeh Pascal/Peter Arnold Inc.; p. 17 © Sandy Buckley/www.iStockphoto.com; p. 19 © Stephen Frink/Getty Images; p. 21 © Heather Perry/Getty Images.

Library of Congress Cataloging-in-Publication Data

Miller, Tori.
  Manta rays / Tori Miller. — 1st ed.
      p. cm. — (Freaky fish)
  Includes index.
  ISBN 978-1-4358-2753-0 (library binding) — ISBN 978-1-4358-3169-8 (pbk.)
ISBN 978-1-4358-3175-9 (6-pack)
  1. Mobulidae—Juvenile literature. I. Title.
  QL638.85.M6M55 2009
  597.3′5—dc22
                                        2008028352

Manufactured in the United States of America

Contents

Meet the Manta Ray

The ocean is calm. Suddenly, a dark, kite-shaped fish jumps 5 feet (1.5 m) out of the water. From fin to fin the giant fish is more than 20 feet (6 m) wide. It is a manta ray! The manta flips in the air and lands with a huge splash that can be heard for miles (km).

Mantas are a type of ray. There are more than 400 different kinds of rays. Manta rays are the biggest of them all. The largest mantas can be as big as 30 feet (9 m) across. That is almost as long as a school bus! Do you want to find out more? Let's dive into the underwater world of this freaky fish!

A manta is shown here as it jumps out of the water. Mantas have been seen jumping three

Manta Rays at Home

Manta rays like warm water. They live in **tropical** seas around the world. Mantas do not spend much time near the bottom of the ocean like other types of rays. Instead, they like to swim near the surface, or top, of the water. Mantas also tend to stay near land. They can often be found in the **shallow** water around rocks and **coral reefs**.

Mantas do not spend much time together. Even when many mantas are together at a good feeding site, they do not pay much attention to each other. Mantas spend most of their lives alone.

Here a manta ray swims over a coral reef. It is believed that manta rays migrate, or move, to

A Blanket Fish?

The **scientific** name for a manta ray is *Manta birostris*. The word "manta" means "cover" or "blanket." The manta ray was given this name because of its large, flat shape. Most mantas are 17 to 22 feet (5–7 m) wide. The biggest mantas can weigh up to 3,000 pounds (1,361 kg).

Mantas have two large, triangular **pectoral fins**. These fins look like large wings. They allow the manta to swim gracefully through the water. Mantas move by softly waving these huge fins. When mantas swim, they look like they are flying through the water.

It is the winglike fins and flat body that give manta rays their name. Mantas are kin to stingrays, but mantas do not have a pointy part on their tails, as stingrays do.

No Bones About It!

Did you know that rays are kin to sharks? It is true! Like sharks' bodies, rays' bodies do not have any bones. Instead of hard bones, rays have soft **cartilage**. They also have bumpy, sandpaper-like skin, just as sharks do.

It is hard to say exactly what color manta rays are, since they are all a bit different. Most mantas are black, grayish blue, or dark brown on top and white underneath. Mantas also have dark spots on their undersides and light markings on their shoulders. Each manta's markings are different. Scientists use the markings to keep track of different mantas.

Here we can see the light underside and black markings on this manta. Many fish have light undersides so enemies below them will not see the fish against the lighter ocean surface.

The Manta Ray: Freaky Facts

○Mantas are sometimes called devilfish because they have fins on their heads that look like horns when they are curled up.

○Manta rays can swim up to 15 miles per hour (24 km/h).

○An adult manta may eat up to 60 pounds (27 kg) of **plankton** and small fish in one day.

○Manta rays have a very good sense of smell.

○A manta ray's brain is about the same size as a cat's brain.

○Manta rays have several rows of small teeth only on their bottom jaws, or mouthparts. They do not use these teeth to feed.

∘No one knows how long mantas live, but scientists think that it is over 20 years.

∘The first baby manta to be born in an aquarium was born in Japan on June 16, 2007.

Big Fish, Little Food

Even though mantas are very large, their food is very small! A manta's main food is **microscopic** plankton. A manta feeds by opening its large mouth and swimming in circles through a place rich with plankton.

A manta has two hornlike fins, called cephalic fins, on either side of its mouth. It uses these fins to direct food into its mouth. Inside the mouth, the water passes through the manta's **gill rakers**, but the food gets stuck there. Mantas also eat small fish, which they swallow whole. Mantas curl up their cephalic fins when they are not eating.

This manta has its mouth open wide to catch plankton and small fish. Its mouth acts like a

Mantas for Dinner

Manta rays are too big to have many enemies. The only animals that hunt and eat mantas are large sharks and orca whales.

People may be the manta's biggest enemy. Mantas have been hunted for their meat and hides. They are hunted for their livers, which are rich in oil. Manta rays are also hunted for their gills, which they use to breathe underwater. Some people use the gills for treating a deadly illness called cancer. Mantas are not an **endangered species** yet. However, if we are not careful, scientists are worried that mantas might soon become endangered.

This is an orca whale, also known as a killer whale. Orcas can be up to 32 feet (10 m) long, and they eat manta rays, sharks, seals, and many other large sea animals.

Cleanup Time!

Manta rays do not have many large enemies, but they do have many very small ones. **Parasites** are small animals that attach, or fix, themselves onto the bodies of larger animals to feed on them, little by little. Too many parasites will make a manta weak and sick.

To fix this problem, mantas visit cleaning stations. Mantas even line up and wait their turns! At these stations, small, colorful fish called wrasses get their dinner while cleaning the parasites and dead skin off the mantas. Other small cleaning fish called remoras have sucker disks that they use to attach themselves to mantas.

This manta ray is giving a ride to a remora. Remoras fix themselves to large rays, sharks, and other fish as a way to keep themselves safe and as a way to get free food!

Manta Babies

Mantas can have babies at any time during the year. It can take up to 13 months for the baby manta to grow inside the mother. Baby mantas are called pups. Most mantas give birth to only one pup at a time, though sometimes they can have two.

Pups are born wrapped in their pectoral fins. They spread their fins and start swimming as soon as they are born. Newborn pups weigh about 24 pounds (11 kg) and have a wingspan of about 3 feet (1 m). Manta pups grow fast. In its first year of life, a manta will double its size!

Male mantas chase female mantas for a long time before they come together to mate. A mother manta will wait a year after giving birth before making another baby.

Please Don't Touch the Mantas

People used to be afraid of manta rays. Today people know these gentle giants are not a danger. Because of this, though, swimmers sometimes try to touch or even ride on mantas. This is not a good idea. We cannot know if mantas want this to happen. Plus, mantas have a coating of **mucus** on their bodies that keeps them safe from illnesses. When people touch mantas, they hurt this coating.

Mantas are fun to watch, though. Imagine seeing a manta when you are in the water! Do not touch them, but feel thankful you saw this fish up close.

Glossary

cartilage (KAHR-tuh-lij) The bendable matter from which people's noses and ears are made and that is also found in sharks and rays.

coral reefs (KOR-ul REEFS) Underwater hills of coral, or hard matter made up of the bones of tiny sea animals.

endangered species (in-DAYN-jerd SPEE-sheez) Kinds of animals that will likely die out if people do not keep them safe.

gill rakers (GIL RAY-kerz) Body parts that some fish use for eating, mostly fish that eat very small fish called plankton.

microscopic (my-kreh-SKAH-pik) Very small.

mucus (MYOO-kus) Thick, slimy matter produced by the body of many animals.

parasites (PER-uh-syts) A living thing that lives in, on, or with another living thing.

pectoral fins (PEK-tuh-rul FINZ) The fins on the side of a fish's body.

plankton (PLANK-ten) Very small plants and animals that drift with water currents.

scientific (sy-un-TIH-fik) Having to do with the study of the world.

shallow (SHA-loh) Not deep.

tropical (TRAH-puh-kul) Having to do with the warm parts of Earth that are near the equator.

Index

A
air, 4
aquarium, 13

B
brain, 12

C
cancer, 16
cartilage, 10
cephalic fins, 14
cleaning stations, 18
coral reefs, 6

E
endangered species, 16

F
fin(s), 4, 8, 14, 20
food, 14

G
gill rakers, 14

M
markings, 10
mucus, 22

N
name, 8

O
ocean, 4, 6

P
parasites, 18
pectoral fins, 8, 20
plankton, 12, 14

S
seas, 6
splash, 4

T
teeth, 12

W
water, 4, 6, 8, 14, 22
wrasses, 18

Web Sites

Due to the changing nature of Internet links, PowerKids Press has developed an online list of Web sites related to the subject of this book. This site is updated regularly. Please use this link to access the list:
www.powerkidslinks.com/ffish/rays/